Cover *24 October 1956: Soviet tanks reach Budapest at the start of the uprising.*

Frontispiece *November 1956: Soviet troops guard the crossroads leading to the Danube Bridge.*

THE HUNGARIAN UPRISING

Alan Blackwood

FLASHPOINTS

The Arab-Israeli Issue
The Conflict in Afghanistan
The Cuban Missile Crisis
The Hungarian Uprising
The Irish Question
The Revolution in Iran
The Rise of Solidarity
The Suez Crisis
The Vietnam War

First published in 1986 by
Wayland (Publishers) Ltd
61 Western Road, Hove
East Sussex BN3 1JD, England

Typeset, printed and bound in Great Britain at
The Bath Press, Avon

British Library Cataloguing in Publication Data

Blackwood, Alan
   The Hungarian uprising.
   1. Hungary—History—Revolution, 1956
   2. Hungary—Politics and government—1945–
   I. Title
   943.9′052   DB957

ISBN 0-85078-729-7

Contents

1
A struggle for liberty

On the morning of 4 November 1956 the Hungarian Prime Minister, Imre Nagy, made the following radio announcement: 'Today at daybreak Soviet forces started an attack against our capital. Our troops are fighting. The government is in its place. I notify the people of our country and the entire world of this fact.'

As he was speaking, a Budapest journalist was on the phone to the Associated Press news agency in Vienna: 'Please tell the world of the treacherous attack against our struggle for liberty. Our troops are already engaged in fighting. Help-Help-Help!'

Another journalist watched from his office window, 'the roar of the Soviet tanks is so loud we can't hear each other's voices. They are firing towards the Danube. Our boys are on the barricades and calling for more arms and ammunition...'

It was the beginning of the end for the Hungarian uprising of 1956. Doomed to failure it may have been, but it shook the world, and tested East-West reaction in the face of confrontation.

Was it a crisis that suddenly erupted, or the result of years of unrest? What made the Hungarians fight so desperately, defending streets and buildings to the last man, woman or child? Why was there an uprising at all, when Hungary was supposed to be such a loyal communist ally of the Soviet Union?

To answer these questions, we need to know something about the Hungarians themselves, and about their long and dramatic past. Their language gives us a clue to their character, their strong sense of pride and independence, of being something apart, even from their closest neighbours. It is not a Slavic tongue, like Russian, Polish or Czech, nor is it in any way related to German, or to Latin, like Romanian. The Hungarian language is inherited from an ancient race

Opposite *Hungarian Prime Minister, Imre Nagy, broadcasts his request for Soviet military withdrawal from Hungary.*

9

called the Magyars, who moved across southern Russia and settled in the region of Hungary in about AD 900.

A history of domination
The land the Magyars settled in was mostly rolling plains, bordered by the Carpathian Mountains in the east, Lake Balaton in the west, and crossed by the River Danube. This was, and still is, ideal land for cattle grazing and growing fruit and grain. Unfortunately, it was also surrounded by, or stood in the way of larger and stronger races and nations. So, from early in their history, the Magyars and then the Hungarians were invaded; and the country's frontiers have changed many times, as a result.

One of Hungary's most formidable enemies of past times were the Ottoman Turks. In 1453, the Turks captured Constantinople (now Istanbul) and advanced from there into Europe, conquering Hungary and occupying it for the next

Opposite *Hungarians demonstrate in eastern Budapest at the beginning of the uprising.*

Below *After capturing Constantinople in 1453, the Turks advanced to Hungary.*

11

two hundred years. An Austrian army finally expelled the Ottoman Turks, only to possess Hungary for themselves as part of the Austrian Empire, ruled from Vienna by the Hapsburgs.

In 1848, during a period of unrest all over Europe, a Hungarian statesman and patriot, Lajos Kossuth, led a revolt against the Austrian rule. The Hapsburg Emperor Franz Joseph called on Tsarist Russia for help and the revolt was crushed, leaving Kossuth an exile for life. In 1867, because of weakening Hapsburg power, Hungary did secure a large degree of self-rule, with the creation of the Austro-Hungarian Empire. But this collapsed in 1918, at the end of the First World War. In the post-war peace settlements, Hungary lost a great deal of territory. On the other hand, the country had become truly independent.

The shaded area on the map (superimposed over modern-day boundaries) indicates the extent of the Austro-Hungarian Empire until 1918.

Independence at last?

The nation enjoyed a brief period of liberal government, but this was quickly overturned by a communist revolution, led by Béla Kun. When this failed in 1920, the leadership fell to Miklos Horthy, who was to continue in office for

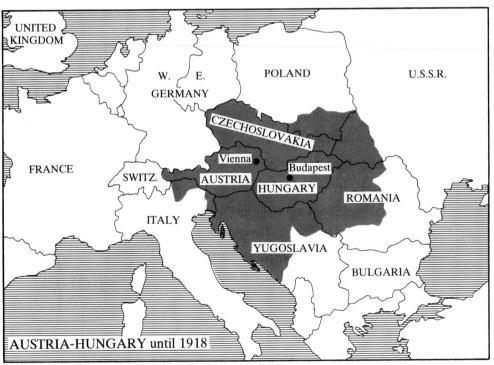

25 years. Horthy, an admiral in the old Austro-Hungarian navy, acted like an authoritarian monarch, deciding policies and imprisoning those who opposed him.

One Hungarian writer described the early years of his rule as 'corrupt and happy-go-lucky'. His government did

Admiral Horthy, the Hungarian regent attending a procession in Budapest. **Inset** *Béla Kun.*

little to change or improve life for the majority of Hungarians, though Budapest itself (the two parts of the city, Buda and Pest, being on opposite banks of the Danube) was full of rich people and was one of the most fashionable cities in Europe. At the same time, history seemed to be repeating itself. By 1933, Hungary was once again trapped between two much stronger powers: in the east the Soviet Union, ruled by Joseph Stalin, and in the west, Nazi Germany, led by Adolf Hitler.

Horthy's fear of communism drew him and his country closer to Germany. Hitler, in his turn, courted Hungary's friendship by handing back some of the territory lost in the 1918 peace settlements. At the outbreak of the Second World War in 1939, Hungary found herself allied to the Axis powers (Hitler's Germany and Mussolini's fascist Italy). German troops used the country, first to launch their attack on Yugoslavia and Greece, and then as a base for their invasion of the Soviet Union.

Hungary was allied to the Axis powers (led by Hitler and Mussolini) at the outbreak of the Second World War.

14

Horthy in exile. Hitler deposed Horthy in 1944.

Germany's early victories in Soviet Russia were good news for Hungary. By 1944, however, with the Soviet Red Army on the advance, Hungary was in grave danger. Horthy tried to negotiate peace agreements with both the western Allies (the United States and Britain) and with the Soviet

Union. Alas, it was too late. Hitler deposed Horthy and annexed the country, filling it with his own troops and the notoriously violent SS police. The war suddenly came home to Hungary with a vengeance. The nation's Jews, who had previously escaped persecution, were rounded up and followed millions of others to SS concentration camps or into forced labour.

Hungary, 1945: a devastated country
As the Red Army made their final advance, the Germans

The Second World War left much of Hungary in ruins.

chose Hungarian soil for one of their last battles. The land was devastated, the towns and cities reduced to ruins, as Germans and Russians fought to the bitter end. 'Man-high rubble covered the streets.' wrote one observer of shattered Budapest. 'The wrecks of thousands of planes, tanks and motor cars were everywhere. Merciful snow covered the uncounted dead.'

At the end of the Second World War, in April 1945, Hungary was in a worse plight than at any time in her long and turbulent history.

2
A divided Europe

The 'Big Three'

In the closing weeks of the Second World War, Hitler hoped that the three principal Allies, the United States of America and Britain on the one hand, the Soviet Union on the other, would suddenly disagree with each other, and so save the Third Reich from final destruction. This did not happen, of course. Hitler committed suicide amid the ruins of Berlin, and Germany surrendered. But he had correctly foreseen the way things were soon to go. The only objective the war-time Allies shared was the defeat of Nazi Germany. Once this was accomplished, substantial rifts in the alliance began to appear.

The United States and Britain were both democracies and basically capitalist in outlook. The Soviet Union was the world's first and most powerful communist state. Before the war brought these countries together as allies, the capitalist nations and the Soviet Union had deeply feared and mistrusted each other. This mutual hostility was always in the background, even when they had taken common cause against Nazi Germany. It was quick to return to the surface.

An Iron Curtain descends

When American and Soviet troops, advancing from opposite directions, met each other in the middle of Germany in 1945, their comradeship was short-lived. Just a year later, Winston Churchill, one of the 'Big Three' Allied leaders, declared that 'an iron curtain has descended across the continent of Europe'. He was referring to the system of mine-fields, barbed-wire fences, armed patrols and check-points that were in the process of sealing off those countries of eastern and central Europe that had been liberated by the Red Army. The Soviet leader, Marshal Joseph Stalin (another of the war-time 'Big Three') was not solely concerned with acquiring new territory. He saw countries like

Opposite *The Iron Curtain between East and West Berlin; one of the many borders dividing Europe.*

19

Romania, Bulgaria, Poland, Czechoslovakia and Hungary as a first line of defence, as 'buffer states', in the event of any future attack by the western capitalist nations.

Hungary's case, in fact, was different from that of her neighbours, for she had been an ally of Nazi Germany. Consequently the Soviet Union, while claiming to be her liberator, also demanded war reparations. Factories built by the Germans were dismantled and their contents, down to the last nut and bolt, were dispatched to the Soviet Union. For weeks on end, long train loads of industrial plant and equipment heading for the Soviet frontier were a common sight. Stalin also demanded large payments in the form of gold and silver reserves. Through 1945 and 1946, Hungary had to give to the Soviet Union far more in money and materials than she could invest in her own economy. As a result, her currency rapidly lost its value, and there was a period of terrible inflation, during which food prices sometimes went up two or three times in a day.

Turning Hungary into a Soviet 'buffer state' or 'satellite nation' took a little longer than some of the other East European countries. For the sake of the war-time alliance, Stalin had agreed with America's President Roosevelt and Britain's Prime Minister Churchill that all the liberated countries of Europe should decide on their own futures through free and democratic elections, once the war was over. Free

Opposite *The USSR and the Warsaw Pact countries.*

NORWAY

SWEDEN

FINLAND

DENMARK

Baltic Sea

USSR

EAST
GERMANY

POLAND

WEST
GERMANY

CZECHOSLOVAKIA

AUSTRIA

HUNGARY

ROMANIA

YUGOSLAVIA

Black Sea

ITALY

BULGARIA

ALBANIA

GREECE

TURKEY

Mediterranean Sea

elections did take place in Hungary in 1946. At these elections, a moderate party, called the Smallholders, won a majority of the votes, and their leader, Ferenc Nagy, headed a coalition government. The new post-war Hungary, despite such problems as inflation, was optimistically described as 'an oasis of culture and liberty'.

Stalin, however, was only biding his time. Hungarian communists, long exiled in Moscow, had all returned home, and were busily getting themselves into positions of power. One of these was Mátyás Rákosi, a staunch admirer of Stalin. Rákosi soon became Ferenc Nagy's deputy in the coalition government, but he saw this merely as a stepping stone to real political power. 'There was one organization', he explained later, 'over which our party demanded full control from the very first moment. This was the State Defence Authority. We kept this organization in our hands from the first day of its establishment.' He was not referring to the army but to a political secret police force, which was of more value to Rákosi than any number of election votes.

Vaczi Street, Budapest 1946: After the war life slowly returned to normal under the Smallholders.

Rákosi's 'salami tactics'

At just about the time that Churchill made his 'Iron Curtain' speech, Rákosi and his Stalinist followers, taking their cue from Moscow, began to act. Using tactics long familiar to those aiming at a political take-over, they sought to smear, to discredit their opponents. They accused the Smallholders Party of harbouring a right-wing conspiracy to overthrow the new republic. The Smallholders' General Secretary was arrested by the Soviet military authorities on the grounds that they were acting to protect the Hungarian constitution. Shortly after, Ferenc Nagy was forced to resign as Prime Minister while he was out of the country, and then exiled. Other opponents were similarly discredited, forced from office or arrested. Rákosi, with a touch of grim humour, described his moves as 'salami tactics'—slicing up the political opposition, piece by piece, like a salami sausage (see page 72).

Mátyás Rákosi, First Secretary of the new constitution, in August 1949.

He next turned against the Catholic Church by arresting its leader in Hungary, Cardinal Mindszenty, and imprisoning him on charges of conspiracy. The head of the Hungarian Lutheran (Protestant) Church was also arrested, for alleged financial fraud.

To secure his personal position of power, Rákosi removed all possible critics from within his own party. His chief victim was the Foreign Minister, László Rajk. He accused Rajk of collaborating with Marshal Tito of Yugoslavia. This was a clever move on Rákosi's part, because Tito, though head of a communist government, had openly spoken out against some Soviet policies. By linking Rajk with Tito, Rákosi was able to have him removed from office, tried for treason and hanged (see page 72).

In Romania, Bulgaria, Poland and Czechoslovakia, events, largely encouraged by the Soviet leadership in Moscow, had taken a similar course. By 1949, each had a communist dictator in charge, some of whom were more compliant to Soviet doctrine than others. In Hungary, Stalin had Rákosi.

Cardinal Mindszenty, Head of the Roman Catholic Church is arrested in 1948.

24

3
A political time bomb

Rákosi had been a sincere communist in his time, serving a long prison sentence for his beliefs during Admiral Horthy's regime. But he now showed himself to be a ruthless dictator. All parties, other than his brand of communism, were, as someone said, 'nothing more than an address in the telephone directory'. The trades unions had no power. Strikes were made illegal, since it was argued that in a 'people's democracy' which served the workers, strike action was self-destructive. A great deal of money was spent on education, but as historian David Pryce-Jones has pointed out, 'indoctrination took up a lot of time and energy. There were active education campaigns against capitalist countries, whose teenagers were pictured as deprived and wretched, or else degenerate. Books were rewritten. Youth organisations met in an almost religious way, singing the *Stalin Cantata*, an official work, in choruses.'

Living in fear of the AVH

To safeguard his position, Rákosi used the AVH, the state

A member of the AVH (secret police) walks casually down a busy street. During the uprising such men were hunted down.

security police. This feared and despised group were more commonly known by Hungarians as the 'Avo'. The size of an army, over a period of five years the AVH arrested, tortured, imprisoned and executed an estimated 150,000 people. Jack-booted and uniformed AVH also carried out tasks where trouble might be expected, such as the forced round-up of kulaks or peasants into collective farms, where they worked not for themselves, but for the state. As a back-up, should it be needed, Red Army units were garrisoned around the country. They were supposed to be in Hungary as guests, but some Hungarians saw them more as an occupying force.

All this had a disastrous effect on the nation's morale. Unrealistic plans for industry and reconstruction made matters worse. Budapest, for example, was to have an underground railway, modelled on the Moscow Metro. But there had been insufficient surveying of the city's sub-soil, the tunnels kept flooding, and the project was abandoned. Rákosi's pro-Soviet stance also led him to gear the country's economy to the needs of the Soviet Union, rather than its own. Vast sums of money were invested in heavy industry, which largely produced goods for the Soviet Union. Farming and agriculture, although more economically viable, were badly neglected. As a result, agricultural production slumped, so that real wages fell too. Many people had been better off even during the war.

By contrast, Rákosi and his colleagues lived in grand style, protected by the AVH. Special shops, filled with luxury goods, were reserved for them. They had their own holiday villas by Lake Balaton, fenced off from the surrounding land. They were driven everywhere in limousines, with curtained windows to shield them from the public gaze. Banners and posters proclaimed, 'Long Live Mátyás Rákosi, Wise Leader Of The Working People!' In truth, he was hated and feared by almost everyone.

Stalin's death in 1953 however, proved to be disastrous for Rákosi. Within three months of the dead leader's funeral, he was summoned to Moscow to face the new collective Soviet leadership of Georgi Malenkov, Nikolai Bulganin and Nikita Khrushchev. They accused him of mis-managing the Hungarian economy, and, worse still, of abusing his position of power. As a result, Rákosi lost the post of Prime Minister to Imre Nagy (no relation to Ferenc Nagy), although he remained First Secretary of the Hungarian communist party.

Opposite *Agricultural development in Hungary was slow during the 1950s. Many farmers still used horses.*

27

Nagy, a long standing member of the Politburo, was very popular with the Hungarian people.

Nagy appointed Prime Minister

Like Rákosi, Imre Nagy had been an early convert to communism, had worked secretly for the party in Hungary before the war, spending a period of exile in the Soviet Union, before returning home again. In appearance and character, though, the two men were very different. Rákosi looked cunning and unscrupulous, while Nagy, with his large moustache and spectacles, appeared much more an honest man of the people, and he was. He had been a long-standing member of Hungary's Politburo, but Rákosi had made sure that he never rose any higher in the government. Now, suddenly, Rákosi was out and Nagy was in.

Rákosi fought back. Policy disputes among the Soviet leaders gave him the chance to rally support within the party, charge Nagy with wanting to destroy communism and oust him again from the government (see page 72). However, it was but a brief victory for the political climate was changing.

In 1955, the more tolerant Soviet leaders met with Marshal Tito, and a reconciliation between the Soviet Union

(see page 72)

Above *Stalin's death in 1953 brought about many changes in communist party policies. Left to right: Malenkov, Bulganin, Khrushchev, Kaganovitch and Mikoyan pay their last respects.*

29

1955: The new Soviet
leadership headed by
Khrushchev (left) re-
established good
relations with Marshal
Tito of Yugoslavia.

and Yugoslavia was achieved. Since 1948 relations between
Yugoslavia and the other communist countries had badly
deteriorated, eventually leading to a complete economic
boycott of the country. Stalin had accused Tito of many
communist heresies, one being his belief that each communist country should decide on its own road to socialism,
free from Soviet influence. By 1955, Tito was able to re-
establish links with Moscow, as well as maintain his
country's independence and friendship with the West. This
was indeed a step towards a more liberal form of communist
understanding.

Rákosi was now in a very awkward position, for he had
continuously attacked Tito's government, and used Tito as

an excuse for eliminating László Rajk. Rajk's widow demanded a pardon for her husband. 'These criminals,' she said bitterly, referring to Rákosi and his henchmen, 'not only murdered László Rajk. They have trampled underfoot all sentiment and honesty in this country. Murderers should not be criticised—they should be punished.'

As if this was not damaging enough, Rákosi next heard Khrushchev, at the Twentieth Congress of the Soviet communist party in Moscow, declare that Stalin had ruled by terror and was guilty of numerous political crimes. Rákosi, as one of Stalin's hand-picked men, was finished. In July 1956 he was summarily dismissed from all his posts within the Hungarian communist party and government, and fled the country to escape arrest.

He left behind him a political time bomb, running on a very short fuse.

László Rajk at his trial in 1949.

4
The uprising begins

At about nine o'clock on the evening of 23 October 1956, the AVH fired on the huge crowd gathered in front of Budapest's Radio Building. It was the start of the Hungarian uprising.

A lot had happened since Rákosi's departure in July. Hungary's new political leader, Ernö Gerö, though one of Rákosi's close former colleagues, had made some welcome changes. He relaxed the compulsory teaching of Russian in schools, curbed the power of the AVH, and lifted some restrictions on foreign travel. The problem he faced, common to all repressive regimes, was that even mild reforms soon increased the people's appetite for more. Once the lid was raised after years of injustice, there was no replacing it. Students were in the forefront of the growing unrest. They demanded the withdrawal of Soviet agencies and Red Army units from the country, the arrest and trial of Rákosi, and free elections.

Other developments, at home and abroad, added fuel to the growing crisis. To try and pacify public opinion, Gerö arranged to have László Rajk's body transferred to Budapest's Kerepes cemetery, where many of the nation's heroes were buried. Instead, the ceremony created a great wave of patriotic feeling, and even more resentment against the government.

Then, in early October, demonstrations erupted in Poland, fuelled by Khrushchev's speech against Stalin. The subsequent riots highlighted the bitter feelings towards the old Stalinist leadership. To everyone's surprise, the Soviet leaders bowed to Polish demands for a new government, headed by the popular and more liberal Vladislav Gomulka. As one journalist pointed out 'To the Hungarians ... there seemed to be no reason why history should not repeat itself—particularly history less than a week old.'

Opposite *A demonstration in Budapest for the withdrawal of Soviet units based in the country.*

Opposite *Hungarians meet peacefully on 23 October at the statue of Joseph Bem.*

The first shots are fired

Events of 23 October in Budapest had started on a fine, sunny autumn afternoon, with a march from the statue of Sandor Petöfi, a Hungarian patriot, to that of the Polish General Josef Bem. The two men had fought side by side in the 1848 uprising against the Austrians and the Russians of Tsar Nicholas, and the march was a demonstration of support for the Poles in their recent dealings with the Soviet Union. At Bem's statue, someone unfurled a Hungarian flag from which the communist emblem of a hammer and an ear of wheat had been removed and the old Hungarian coat-of-arms put in its place. It was the first of many such flags to be seen all over the country in the next few days.

1982: Polish people meet to commemorate the many workers killed in Poland's struggle for greater freedom in 1956. The success of the Poles in 1956 gave renewed hope to Hungarian rebels.

34

From the statue the crowd, growing in number all the time, moved back across the Danube to the Parliament Building, its great dome rising high above the river. It was getting dark by then, but word spread that the Politburo, sensing a crisis, was in session. The crowd waited expectantly. Someone inside the building ordered the street lamps to be switched off, hoping the crowd would disperse. Instead, there were cries of 'We've had enough of darkness!' People found newspapers, made them up into bundles and lit them. Forming a great torchlight procession, they moved on through the streets to the Radio Building, where Gerö was due to make a broadcast. It was heavily guarded by the AVH secret police.

'We rushed up to the Avos, who were pointing their guns at us,' recalled one member of the crowd afterwards. 'They were obviously petrified that we might attack them. We were desperate and some of us began to plead with them. "Aren't you ashamed of yourselves, pointing guns at your fellow Hungarians? Weren't you born of Hungarian fathers and mothers like ourselves?"'

Apparently, some of the AVH lowered their guns. Others panicked. Shots were fired killing several people in the crowd, followed by tear gas bombs, lobbed from windows of the Radio Building. It was the signal for an armed insurrection. 'From that moment,' concluded a United Nations report, 'bloodshed was inevitable' (see page 73).

The remains of the Magyar Radio Building. From here the AVH first fired on the crowd below.

The government immediately called out the army. It was their first big mistake. The soldiers—Hungarians, not Russians—went over to the insurgents almost to a man. So did the ordinary police. Colonel Kopacsi, chief of the Budapest Police Force, at first believed the insurgents to be

A Hungarian soldier with a young insurgent.

fascists and middle-class reactionaries, as Radio Budapest had reported them to be. It was only after arresting some young boys that Kopacsi realised that they were hopeful young communists. They were not against communism as the western media preferred to portray at the time, they were fighting for Hungarian sovereignty, and a more liberal form of independent communism, less dominated by Soviet policy. Kopacsi knew that if the insurgents were to stand a chance he must actively support them. Weapons and ammunition were distributed. Factory workers got hold of trucks and vans. Within hours the Hungarian capital was virtually in the hands of armed bands of self-styled freedom

Young Hungarian women played an important part in the fighting against Soviet troops.

Insurgents toppled the massive statue of Stalin using blowlamps. **Left** *The statue is broken off at the knees.* **Below** *The head of the statue bears a road sign.*

fighters. They engaged in fighting with the AVH who were still defending the Radio Building. They captured the offices of the government-sponsored newspaper *Szabad Nép*, after further fighting with the AVH. Across the city, another crowd was toppling the massive bronze statue of Stalin. Metal workers with blow lamps broke it off at the knees, so that two large bronze boots were all that remained on the marble base. The head was severed too, and left in the street with a traffic sign tied across it reading 'Dead End!'

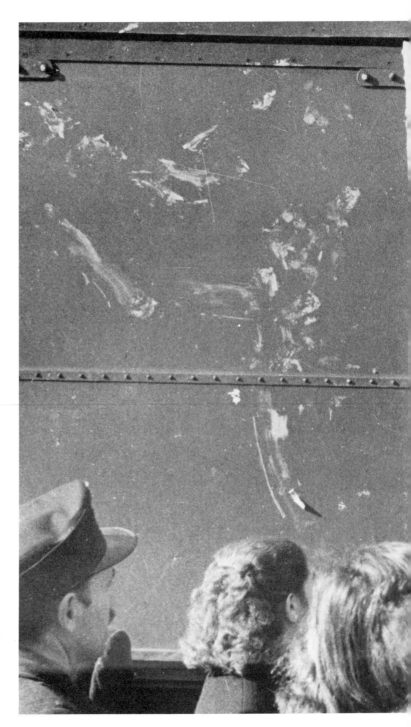

Many posters and leaflets were distributed during the uprising. This one, attached to the side of a tramcar is entitled 'The Russians at the door'.

Soviet tanks reach Budapest

Early next day the first Soviet tanks, from their depots about 40 kilometres away, reached Budapest. They took up strategic positions by the bridges across the Danube and moved up and down the main streets, but they could not curtail the freedom fighters. The latter, for their part, lacked an overall command or plan of action, as one Hungarian professor explained to the United Nations after the uprising—'It was unique in history that the Hungarian revolution had no leaders. It was not organized... The will for freedom was the moving force in every action.' They operated in small groups, attacking the tanks when and where they

Soviet tanks reach Kosztarszag Square on 24 October 1956.

could, darting out from side streets and alleyways to try and damage their tracks, or more daringly, jump onto them and throw Molotov cocktails (petrol bombs) or shoot into the command hatch. Tragically some of the fighters were little more than children, but their ingenuity was astounding. Soup plates were turned over and placed across the road to resemble mines. Any tank that hesitated was lost. One eye-witness watched several youngsters creep up on a tank. 'Suddenly they jumped onto the tank, one of them produced a pistol and shot into it, while the rest stole the machine gun of the Russian driver. Then they fled down the street under a hail of fire from the other Russian tanks.'

To hinder the Soviet tanks, soup plates were laid across the road. Some were simply to resemble mines, while others contained explosive charges.

Opposite *Hungarian insurgents capture the AVH building. They have removed the communist emblem from their flags.*

The village of Magyarovar burying those who were killed while attending an agricultural meeting.

Magyarovar: the AVH massacre

There was fighting in other towns and cities, in Gyór, Debrecen, Sopron, Szeged, Pecs. In the small country town of Magyaróvár, there was terrible carnage when the AVH threw grenades and machine-gunned a peaceful agricultural meeting, killing 82 defenceless men, women and children. 'News of the massacre,' said Noel Barber, a British journalist in Hungary throughout the uprising, 'switched the fury of the insurgents from the Russians back to the AVH. They were hunted down like animals, hung on trees, or just beaten to death by passers-by. The rage of the insurgents was intensified when they found pay slips in Avo pockets showing that officers were earning 9000 forints a month—eleven times the wage of an average worker. When an Avo was

Many railway coaches and trams were wrecked during the street fighting with the Soviet troops.

killed, the pay slip was pinned to his body. Any money in his pockets was usually burned. Their Poboda (Russian-made) cars were set on fire.'

Budapest soon appeared a war-torn city again. 'Hardly a stretch of tramrail was left,' wrote Noel Barber. 'Hundreds of yards of paving stones had been torn up, the streets were littered with burnt-out cars. I counted the carcasses of at least forty Soviet tanks.' Many of these had been destroyed assaulting the city's Kilian Barracks, which was defended by a rebel contingent of Hungarian troops commanded by Colonel Pál Maléter. Maléter had gone to the barracks with orders to break the resistance of the revolutionaries; instead he became the military force behind the uprising.

5
Warsaw Pact in jeopardy

The outcome of the uprising was decided in one hectic week, between Saturday 27 October and Saturday 3 November. Imre Nagy, still the country's most trusted political figure, had been recalled as Prime Minister. Though a communist, he agreed to form a coalition government along with members of the revived Smallholders and other non-communist parties. He promoted Maléter to the rank of General and to the post of Minister of Defence, hoping thereby to control the freedom fighters and stop the drift towards anarchy. He met with two of the Soviet deputy premiers, Anastas Mikoyan and Mikhail Suslov, who flew in from

General Pál Meléter (left), the military force behind the uprising, discusses defence plans with other officials.

Moscow to assess the situation for themselves. How far, Nagy wanted to know, would the Soviet leaders accede to the people's demands for a free press and radio, and free elections?

The question of Soviet withdrawal

Above all, there was the burning question of the withdrawal of Soviet armed forces. Would they go, or wouldn't they? At one point the tanks did withdraw from Budapest. A press agency reported: 'Soviet tanks crunched out of this war-battered capital today, their red stars still visible through the grime of gunpowder, oil and blood. Then came motor-cycles and trucks. On the back of one truck lay the corpse of a Soviet soldier, his eyes staring vacantly back at the Hungarian capital.'

There was a lull in the fighting, in Budapest and elsewhere, as more Soviet units pulled back. Was the Red Army really going? Had they won?

The Soviet army suffered heavy casualties in the fighting. A Soviet soldier lies in the debris, his body covered with disinfectant to safeguard against the spread of disease.

49

30 October Declaration

Khrushchev realised that the Soviet involvement in Hungary had already damaged East-West relations, particularly since the world press were now in the midst of the crisis. He also knew that if he acceded to all the insurgents demands, he would 'lose face' among the other satellite nations. Opposition from within the Kremlin toward the new 'soft line' approach was another factor to consider. However, Khrushchev held his ground and on 30 October a Soviet declaration was issued. It was an understanding and brave declaration on the part of the Soviet government, beginning with,

> 'The unchangeable foundation of Soviet foreign relations has been and remains a policy of peaceful coexistence, of friendship, and of collaboration with all other states.'

It went on,

> 'In order to insure the mutual security of the socialist countries, the Soviet Government is prepared to review with the other socialist countries signing the Warsaw Pact the question of Soviet troops stationed on the territory of the above-mentioned countries (i.e. Hungary, Romania and Poland).'

In April 1956, Bulganin and Khrushchev met with the British Prime Minister Anthony Eden to discuss East–West relations. Such positive moves were damaged by the events in Hungary later in the year.

This was to prove but a brief respite for the Hungarians. Nagy knew too well the dangers that confronted his government. The insurgents, having succeeded in gaining some of their demands, became increasingly confident, pushing for more and more concessions. Soviet bookshops were broken into and books, magazines and posters were burnt in the street. The situation was further aggravated by some rather irresponsible radio broadcasts on Radio Free Europe, based in Munich. Radio Free Europe was financed partly by funds from the Central Intelligence Agency in America,

A Red Cross truck tours Hungary's war-torn streets searching for injured rebels.

While Imre Nagy pleaded for calm, the insurgents' demands grew. Here they are seen by a captured Soviet tank outside the Parliament Buildings in Budapest.

and its workforce included over 90 Hungarian refugees who had fled from Hungary after the Second World War and the rise of communism. As John O'Kearney wrote in 1957, 'During the days of the fighting it (Radio Free Europe) played a large part in keeping the blood flowing'. For the freedom fighters it was the only source of news—a link with the outside world. One broadcast included how to make Molotov cocktails, and another reported 'The Ministry of Defence and the Ministry of the Interior are still in communist hands. Do not let this continue freedom fighters.'

Nagy, by contrast, pleaded for calm—'Do not demand too much or we will lose everything we have gained'.

UN fail to respond

The exact reasons for the re-mobilization of Soviet troops along the border with Hungary will never be known. Perhaps the Kremlin felt Nagy was losing control of the situation. The Soviets themselves said they were routine manoeuvres. Nobody believed that. Nagy's dread seemed to be coming true. He contacted the Soviet ambassador, Yuri Andropov and threatened to pull Hungary out of the Warsaw Pact if troops re-entered Budapest. He also cabled the United Nations headquarters in New York and asked the Secretary General, Dag Hammerskjold, if the UN would guarantee Hungarian neutrality (see page 71). This move started a fresh wave of rumours and kindled new hope among the freedom fighters. A car with a UN sticker on the windscreen was eagerly stopped by freedom fighters. When the driver told them he was only a member of the UN press corps, one fighter said bitterly, 'Not enough!' In fact, due to several bureaucratic mistakes at the UN, Hammerskjold did not acknowledge this important plea for a whole day, by which time it was too late.

The Soviet leaders may have been ready to negotiate with Nagy on the same kind of terms that had recently settled the crisis in Poland. What must suddenly have hardened their attitude was Nagy's talk of Hungarian neutrality and of taking his country out of the Warsaw Pact. Any threat to its strength and organization was a threat to the security of the Soviet Union itself. It could not be tolerated. Besides, the Soviet leaders must have argued, the situation was already far worse than in Poland. The uprising would have to be crushed.

Opposite *Young Hungarians burn books from a Soviet bookshop.*

Maléter is arrested

On the evening of Saturday 3 November, the Soviet authorities on the spot invited General Maléter to their army headquarters. Apparently they wanted to discuss details of a military withdrawal. Maléter was warned it might be a trap, but decided that was a risk he had to take.

'Everything appeared to go off perfectly in the office where the talks were taking place,' said one of his adjutants afterwards. 'Then, towards midnight about twenty Soviet military police in green caps burst into the room and covered our delegation with their guns. I was watching our boss. The others were pale. Only his face didn't change. "So that's it, is it?" he said to the Russians, standing up calmly. I seized my own sten gun, thinking that before dying I would still shoot a few rounds at the men in green caps, but the boss called out, "Stop it. It's useless to resist." What could I do? His words were my orders and I let my sten gun be taken away.'

General Maléter was arrested just as fresh Soviet divisions were pouring into the country.

New Soviet divisions enter Hungary on 3 November 1956.

6
'Light is failing'

So we come to the early hours of Sunday 4 November, to the brief statement of what was happening, broadcast over Free Radio Kossuth by Prime Minister Nagy, and to the cries for help, quoted at the start of this narrative.

The Soviet forces mobilized at the beginning of the uprising had not always been sure of their task, or happy with what they were called upon to do. Many of the men had been stationed in Hungary for some time and made friends with the people. There were reports of fraternisation between them and the insurgents. The new Soviet armoured columns now racing towards Budapest and the other large towns were a different proposition. They came fresh to the job from Czechoslovakia, Romania, and from the Soviet Union itself. Their orders were simply to crush the uprising and stamp out resistance, as quickly as possible.

According to Dora Scarlett, who worked for the English language section of Hungarian Radio, many of the men were misled about the nature of their mission. They were going to fight 'fascists, landlords and capitalists', not Hungarian workers, students and soldiers. Some were told they were going to Berlin, not Budapest. On the other hand, as Noel Barber made clear, 'their officers, in their long, grey-waisted coats, were professionals of the first order, who went about their task of subduing the country in a way that left no room for sentiment. They were merciless. If one lone sniper fired a single bullet, retribution was swift and inevitable. Half a dozen tanks rolled up to the building from where the shot had been fired and obliterated it.'

Peter Fryer, another British journalist, wrote of the renewed fighting: 'The battle spared neither civilians nor those bringing aid to the wounded. Bread queues were fired upon, and I saw a man of about seventy lying dead outside a bread shop, the loaf of bread he had just bought still in his hand. Someone had half covered the body with the red, white and green flag.'

Heroic resistance: 'We win or we fall'

The Hungarians grimly resisted, fighting from street to street, house to house. Those still inside the Kilian Barracks held out for another three days, until the last forty survivors were all killed, mown down by machine gun fire as they stumbled out of the ruined building. Facing it across Ulloi Street was the Corvin Cinema, another scene of grim resistance. 'The defenders,' said Noel Barber, 'had captured an anti-tank gun from a disabled Soviet vehicle. They placed it against the steps of the cinema, with an improvised automatic mechanism so they could fire it from inside the building. Not until the cinema was finally shelled with heavy self-propelled artillery, was it evacuated.' Ordinary citizens, in a frenzy of despair, sometimes attacked the tanks and armoured cars with sticks and stones, even with their bare hands.

Freedom fighters took to the hills when they were driven out of the towns. 'We bivouacked on various ridges of the Pilis, Vertes and Bakony Mountains while Soviet helicopters hovered overhead, tracking our line of retreat. Anxiously we listened to foreign broadcasts, waiting and hoping for an eventual change that somehow at some point would force the Soviet Union to negotiate with Imre Nagy after all.'

They waited in vain. The calls for outside help grew more desperate and hopeless. 'Civilised people of the world! We implore you in the name of justice, freedom and the binding moral principle of active solidarity to help us. Our ship is sinking. Light is failing. The shadows grow darker every hour over the soil of Hungary. Listen to our cry, civilized people of the world, and act. Extend us your fraternal aid.'

Opposite *The University buildings in Budapest provided a hiding place for the insurgents.*

Below *As the new Soviet divisions arrived, many insurgents fled to the country regions of Hungary.*

'A terrible festival of death'

As that broadcast was going out, workers joined freedom fighters for a last-ditch stand outside the big industrial suburb of Csepel, near Budapest. They fought and died till their ammunition ran out. By the evening of Friday 9 November the battle was over. 'The smell of stone dust and fire hung in the air ...' wrote Dora Scarlett, 'the dust looked like fog. Over all hung the flags, as though the city was keeping some terrible festival of death. There were more black flags than ever. There were more graves in the parks and squares. There was a constantly changing crowd of people round them, relatives, friends, and ordinary passers-by came to stand for a few minutes in silence, and many were in tears.'

The correspondent of the French newspaper *Le Figaro* cabled home: 'The Red Army now occupies Budapest. It is red with the blood of the workers.'

Hungarians place candles by the body of a young insurgent killed in the fighting.

7
The uprising is crushed

As Hungary counted the cost—an estimated 25,000 dead, Budapest and other towns and cities once more in ruins—another event took precedence in the world press. On 5 November 1956 British and French forces attacked Egypt, in collaboration with an Israeli offensive. The governments of Anthony Eden in London and Jean Monnet in Paris had been planning the attack in secret, ever since Egypt's President Nasser nationalized the Suez Canal. The Americans promptly condemned the action, and after some hesitation, Britain and France agreed on a cease-fire (see page 73). Thus the Suez Crisis had cornered the headlines and diverted world attention, just at the moment when the Soviet armour was pounding its way back into the centre of Budapest. It seemed to the Hungarians the cruellest blow of all.

Suez takes precedence
But had the Suez Crisis made any difference to their own fate? Outside help would have depended on the initiative of the United States, and the American government, in the last analysis, was not prepared to intervene. The two superpowers, for all their cold war hostility, both had their global 'spheres of influence' which they tacitly agreed to respect, for fear of real war breaking out between them. Hungary was within the Soviet sphere of influence, and that was that, in the context of world politics. The American President Eisenhower admitted as much. 'Hungary could not be reached by any of the United Nations or United States units without traversing neutral territory. Sending troops into Hungary through hostile or neutral territory would have involved us in a general war.'

So, with or without the Suez Crisis, the Hungarian uprising was almost bound to fail. All Suez did was to turn the spotlight away from what was happening in Hungary and so save the Soviet Union some embarrassment. Even so, the USSR sank very low in world opinion. In Brussels and

Opposite *1968:*
Czechs demonstrate
against Soviet military
units based in their
country. Similar events
in other European
'satellite' states, before
and after the Hungarian
uprising, has led the
Soviet Union to assess
its' role in regard to
these countries.

Below *Western media*
attention was diverted
from Hungary when
British, French and
Israeli forces invaded
Egypt in October–
November 1956.

Bonn, students demonstrated outside the Soviet embassy. In The Hague tradesmen stopped deliveries to Soviet diplomats, and in Rotterdam dockers refused to handle Soviet ships. Communist parties everywhere lost members.

The official Soviet Party line was that the Red Army had been called in to defend the Hungarian people against a fascist or capitalist-inspired counter-revolution. Nikita Khruschev said: 'We had strength and right on our side, but it was difficult to make a decision because part of the workers were on the side of the counter-revolution. Bullets do not choose between class enemies and misguided workers. Believe me, we spent painful days and nights before coming to a decision.' He was admitting that the uprising had really worried the Soviet leadership (see page 73). There have been, over the years, a series of crises between the Soviet Union and her European 'satellites': East Germany, 1953; Poland, 1956; Czechoslovakia, 1968; Poland again, 1983. But it was the violent events of October and November 1956 that came closest to shaking the foundations of Soviet power.

8
Counting the cost

Imre Nagy, General Maléter, and other members of the revolutionary government sought asylum in the Yugoslav embassy. After written agreements between Tito and Kádár (the new Hungarian Prime Minister) ensured the group's safety, it was arranged for them to be transported to Yugoslavia. This never happened. To everybody's surprise the bus that arrived to escort them was driven by Soviet police. Instead of Yugoslavia, the group were taken to Romania. Eighteen long months later the Hungarian people learnt of their comrades' terrible fate. Both Nagy and Maléter had been executed, the others sentenced to various terms of imprisonment. Shortly before his death Nagy said 'If my life is needed to prove that not all communists are enemies of the people, I gladly make the sacrifice'.

Thousands of Hungarians left the country, mostly for Austria. 'Many of these refugees,' wrote David Pryce-Jones, 'were talented and ambitious and Hungary could ill afford to lose them. Perhaps the government thought that if such people were discontented it would be safer to let them go and not risk another internal explosion.'

After the uprising some insurgents were tried for resisting Soviet intervention.

Kádár: a new tolerance?

János Kádár revived the hated AVH and reintroduced collective farms. Slogans and messages chalked up on walls expressed, in words of bitter sarcasm, what most people thought of him. 'Wanted: Premier for Hungary. Qualifications: no sincere convictions. No backbone. Ability to read or write not required, but must be able to sign documents drawn up by others. Applications should be made to Messrs.

Many Hungarians left the country after the crisis. These men arrived in Austria on Christmas Eve 1956.

The Austro-Hungarian border is repaired by Hungarian soldiers.

Khrushchev and Bulganin.'

Nevertheless, Kádár and the Soviet leaders had learnt some lessons. A favourite slogan of domineering leaders is, 'He who is not for us, is against us'. They demand unquestioning loyalty. Kádár reversed this slogan, and declared, 'He who is not against us, is with us'. This was far more tolerant. So long as people did not actively oppose the state, he implied, they would be left in peace. The Soviet Union reduced its own demands on the Hungarian economy, so allowing living standards to rise.

Today, thirty years later, the cold war and the arms race between the two superpowers are as depressingly alive and intense as ever. But Hungary herself can claim to enjoy the highest standard of living, and the most liberal social and cultural life of any Soviet-bloc country. So, balanced against the terrible loss of life on both sides, perhaps it can be argued that the events in 1956 did have some positive effect on the development of Hungarian society, which could not be forseen at the time the uprising was crushed.

Overleaf *The youth of Hungary today. The country now enjoys a quite liberal social and cultural life.*

Below *János Kádár, the new Prime Minister, meets with Hungarians in 1958.*

Chronology of dates

1918	End of Austro-Hungarian Empire. Hungary proclaimed a republic.
Mar. 1919	Communist revolution led by Béla Kun.
Nov. 1919	Kun's communist regime ends.
Mar. 1920	Admiral Horthy is elected regent.
1939	Horthy signs anti-Comintern Pact with Germany and Hungary leaves the League of Nations.
1941	Hungary declares war on the Soviet Union.
1944	Germany occupies Hungary and Horthy is forced into exile.
1945	Germany surrenders and the Soviet Union occupies Hungary.
	Free elections are held, Ferenc Nagy of the Smallholders Party is proclaimed president.
1949	Ferenc Nagy is deposed and communist government installed, led by Mátyás Rákosi.
	Cardinal Mindszenty is sentenced to life imprisonment for refusing to nationalize the Roman Catholic education system.
Oct. 1949	Lászlá Rajk, a leading 'nationalist' communist is executed.
1950	State security police (the AVH) are created.
	Collectivization of farms is implemented.
	Five-year plan begins with large investment in heavy industry. (Industrial output increases to 37% above pre-war level.) Agricultural production is neglected.

1953	Death of Stalin. Rákosi replaced as Premier by Imre Nagy. Nagy releases political prisoners and peasants are allowed to leave collective farms.
1955	Imre Nagy is forced to resign, Rákosi reinstated as the Party's first secretary.
May 1955	Hungary becomes a signatory of the Warsaw Treaty Organization.
July 1955	Rákosi is formally dimissed from the communist party by Khrushchev, and Erno Gero is appointed first secretary.
	Growing unrest in the country, students demand the trial of Rákosi and withdrawal of Soviet army units garrisoned in Hungary.
1956	
23 Oct.	AVH fire on crowd gathered outside Budapest's Radio Building.
24 Oct.	Soviet tanks reach Budapest.
25 Oct.	Nagy is re-appointed Prime Minister, and tries to negotiate for the withdrawal of Soviet troops.
27 Oct.	Soviet army withdraw from capital.
30 Oct.	Khrushchev's declaration.
1 Nov.	Nagy forms a coalition government including some non-communists.
	Re-mobilization of Soviet troops along Hungary's border. Nagy cables UN and repudiates Warsaw Treaty.
3 Nov.	Fresh Soviet divisions move into Hungary. The uprising is crushed.
4 Nov.	New government is formed led by János Kádár.
1958	Imre Nagy and other members of the uprising are tried and executed.

Appendix I

Imre Nagy's note to Hammerskjold, Secretary General of the United Nations on 1 November 1956

'Reliable reports have reached the Government of the Hungarian People's Republic that further Soviet units are entering into Hungary. (The Prime Minister) summoned M. Andropov, the Soviet Ambassador, and expressed his strongest protest against the entry of further Soviet troops into Hungary. He demanded the instant and immediate withdrawal of these Soviet forces.

'He informed the Soviet Ambassador that the Hungarian Government immediately repudiates the Warsaw Treaty, and, at the same time, declares Hungary's neutrality, turns to the United Nations, and requests the help of the great powers in defending the country's neutrality.

'Therefore I request Your Excellency promptly to put on the agenda of the forthcoming General Assembly of the United Nations the question of Hungary's neutrality and the defence of this neutrality by the four great powers....'

It was signed: 'Imre Nagy, President of the Council of Ministers of the Hungarian People's Republic, designated Minister of Foreign Affairs.'

Appendix II

This book gives the author's view of the background and events leading to the Hungarian uprising in 1956. Naturally, this is largely a 'Western' opinion. In order to present a balanced viewpoint, the Publishers contacted the Hungarian Embassy in London and invited their comments. The following extracts are taken from *Hungary on the Road of Socialist construction 1948–1958*, supplied by the Embassy and represent the 'official' view of events in the autumn of 1956.

On Rákosi's regime:

'Success had dazzled the leaders. The personality cult that gradually enveloped Mátyás Rákosi, the general secretary of the party, altered the leadership style that had been pursued. The principle of collective leadership was violated, the Leninist norms of party life were transgressed ... criticism was squelched within the party. Mátyás Rákosi came to be regarded as 'the infallible sage'.'

On the trial of László Rajk:

'One of the most tragic consequences was that revolutionary law and order were violated. This began with the contrived trial started against László Rajk and his associates in 1949 ... These trials deepened the contradictions which developed in the wake of a practical policy that had slipped to the wrong lane.'

In response to Imre Nagy:

'Imre Nagy's programme created a favourable basis for all oppositionist, enemy, counter-revolutionary and anti-socialist forces ... All the opponents and enemies of the workers power used in their propaganda the mistakes committed by the party leadership. They used in this way also the criticism voiced at the 20th Congress about Stalin and the cult around his person. They used the violations of legality in Hungary ... to increase the moral shock and the ideological and political confusion ... to win over the masses and turn them against the whole system.'

Of the uprising itself:

'All the organizations of the counter-revolution [the term used by the Soviet government for the uprising] ... encouraged by the extensive co-operation of the Western radio stations, began a frantic campaign of incitement against the state security detachments and the Soviet units that supported them. On 23 October, the various right-wing centres organized a demonstration demanding that the AVH should be disbanded and that Soviet troops should leave the country. One of their armed groups, from concealed positions near the roof of the Ministry of Agriculture, opened fire on the crowds demonstrating in front of the House of Parliament, and immediately the right-wing elements spread the lie that "the AVH are shooting at the people".'

Soviet intervention in comparison with the Suez crisis:

'The aggression in Egypt by these two NATO Powers [Britain and France] and their Israeli accomplices showed very many people that these Powers were not adherent to national independence.'

A final conclusion of events ...

'The events of October 1956 brought into focus the fact that the counter-revolutionary forces, receiving many-sided support from the Western imperialist powers and utilizing the mistakes committed by the communist party ... might endanger the people's power.'

Source: *Hungary on the Road of Socialist construction 1948–1958* (Chapters from the History of the Hungarian Workers' Movement).

Glossary

AVH Initials of the *Allamvédelmi Hivatal*, the name of the Hungarian political or secret police. Commonly known to Hungarians as the 'Avo'.

Capitalism Economic system based on the private ownership of the means of production. Workers receive wages for their services, but have no share in the ownership, profits or organization of the workplace.

Coalition A government formed by representatives from two or more political parties.

Communism Political creed founded on the ideas of the German philosopher Karl Marx; based on the collective ownership of the means of production. Each member of the community works for the common benefit according to his capacity and receives according to his needs.

Democracy From the Greek word *demos* meaning 'the people'; a system of government based on the choice of the majority through free elections.

Dictator Political or military leader who assumes complete power. His policies are not restricted by the law.

Fascism The word comes from the Latin *fasces*, describing an axe surrounded by rods, the symbol of Roman authority. Fascism is a political system based on nationalism and dominance of the military. Its authoritarian nature is fundamentally opposed to democracy and liberalism.

First World War (1914–1918) Main belligerents: British Commonweath and Empire, French Empire, United States of America, Russian Empire, Italy (the Allies); German Empire, Austro-Hungarian Empire (the Central Powers).

Kremlin Old Russian name for any fortified city, but now meaning specifically the Moscow Kremlin, which houses the principal departments of government of the Soviet Union.

NATO (North Atlantic Treaty Organization). An international organization composed of the USA, Canada, Iceland, Britain and 11 other European countries. Established in 1949 for the purpose of collective security.

Nazi A member of the National Socialist German Workers' Party. The 'Nazi' Party seized political control of Germany in 1933, under Adolf Hitler.

Politburo Abbreviation for Political Bureau, the policy-making committee of a communist party.

Second World War (1939–1945) Main belligerents: British Commonwealth, United States of America, Soviet Union, France (the Allies); Germany, Austria, Italy, Hungary, Japan (the Axis Powers).

Socialism A system of government similar to communism, but along more moderate lines, whereby the means of production are owned by the community. It is characterized by production for use rather than profit and by the equal distribution of wealth.

Sovereignty A term used in political theory, basically meaning a state's right under international law to be free from legal or political control by any other state.

Soviet Union Usual form of reference to the Union of Soviet Socialist Republics (USSR). Many people mistakenly speak of Russia when they mean the Soviet Union; Russia is only a part of the Soviet Union.

Stalinist A follower of the policies and methods associated with Joseph Stalin.

Third Reich Hitler's name for the 'Greater Reich', composed of all German-speaking people, and comprising of Germany itself, Austria and parts of Czechoslovakia and Poland.

Tsar Russian name for king or emperor. The Tsars ruled the Russian Empire up until the Bolshevik Revolution of 1917, which founded the Soviet Union.

United Nations International organization, with headquarters in New York City, dedicated to preserving world peace. Created in 1945, at the end of the Second World War as a successor to the League of Nations.

Warsaw Pact Treaty of 'friendship, co-operation and mutual aid', but primarily a military alliance between the Soviet Union and Bulgaria, Czechoslovakia, East Germany, Hungary, Poland and Romania. Created in 1955 in response to the Western military alliance of NATO.

Further Reading

General

MICHENER, J. *The bridge at Andau* (Corgi, 1984)

POPESCU, J. *Let's visit Hungary* (Burke, 1985)

PORTER, M. *The Paper Bridge: a return to Budapest* (Quartet, 1981)

RIGBY, B. *The Western Alliance* (Wayland, 1979)

Hungarian history

ISTVAN, D. *The lawful revolution: Louis Kossuth and the Hungarians*

Hungary and the Soviet Union

GIBSON, M. *The Communist Bloc* (Wayland, 1979)

KERTESZ, S. *Between Russian and the West: Hungary and the illusions of peacemaking 1945–1947* (University of Notre Dame Press, 1984)

MEIKLEJOHN TERRY, S. (ed) *Soviet Policy in Eastern Europe* (Yale University Press, 1984)

SCHOPFLIN, G. (ed) *The Soviet Union and Eastern Europe* (Muller, Blond and White, 1986)

Hungary 1956

BARBER, N. *Seven Days of Freedom: the Hungarian Uprising* (Macmillan, 1974)

BUDAPEST PRESS AGENCY, *Hungary on the Road of Socialist construction 1948–1958* (MTI Printing Office, 1981)

FEHER, F. *1956 Revisited* (Allen & Unwin, 1983)

IRVING, D. *Uprising* (Hodder & Stoughton, 1980)

KADAR, J. *Kadar* (Pergamon Press, 1983)

LOMAX, B. (ed) *Eyewitness in Hungary: the Soviet invasion of 1956* (Spokesman Books, 1980)

PRICE-JONES, D. *The Hungarian Revolution* (Ernest Benn, 1969)

TRORY, E. *Hungary 1919 and 1956: the anatomy of counter-revolution* (Crabtree Press, 1981)

Hungary today

HEINRICH, H. *Hungary: politics, economics and society* (Pinter, 1986)

VOLGYES, I. *Hungary: a nation of contradictions* (Bowker, 1985)

Index

Picture acknowledgements

Associated Press 8, 25, 31, 36, 39, 43, 44, 46, 47, 48, 51, 52–53, 59, 64, 65; BBC Hulton Picture Library 11; Camera Press 68; Ginette Laborde 56; Imperial War Museum 14; Interfoto MTI (Budapest) 24, 35, 67; John Hillelson 10, 23, 28 (below), 33, 37, 38, 40–41, 42, 45, 49, 54, 60, 66; Popperfoto 16–17, 20, 22, 62; Rex Features 34; Tim Sharman 26; TOPHAM 13 (both), 15, 18, 28–29 (above), 30, 50, 58, 63. The maps on pages 12 and 21 were supplied by Malcolm S. Walker.